Finding

Bethlehem

In the Midst of **Bedlam**

Finding
Bethlehem
In the Midst of Bedlam

An Advent Study for Adults

James W. Moore

Questions, Prayer, and Focus for the Week Devotions
by Pamela Dilmore

Abingdon Press/Nashville

FINDING BETHLEHEM IN THE MIDST OF BEDLAM
AN ADVENT STUDY FOR ADULTS
Copyright © 2013 by Abingdon Press

This book is printed on acid-free paper.

Library of Congress Cataloging-in-Publication Data

Moore, James W. (James Wendell), 1938-
Finding Bethlehem in the midst of bedlam / James W. Moore.
    p. cm
  ISBN 978-1-4267-6082-2 (pbk. : alk. paper)
  1. Advent—Prayers and devotions. I. Title.
  BV40.M6385 2013
  242'.33—dc23

                                                              2013008500

Scripture quotations in this publication, unless otherwise indicated, are from
the *New Revised Standard Version of the Bible*, copyright 1989, Division of
Christian Education of the National Council of the Churches of Christ in the
United States of America. Used by permission. All rights reserved.

Cover design: Keely Moore

Interior design: Ken Strickland

13 14 15 16 17 18 19 20 21 22—10 9 8 7 6 5 4 3 2 1

MANUFACTURED IN THE UNITED STATES OF
AMERICA

Contents

Introduction:

Bethlehem Always Happens
in the Midst of Bedlam

Let's just admit it: Christmas for many people means uproar, busyness, and wild confusion. It is absolute bedlam! Frayed nerves, emotional tensions, physical exhaustion, unpaid bills, long lines, traffic jams, difficult decisions, and hectic schedules all combine to make the Christmas season a time of busy confusion for many people. How many times in the next few days will we hear people say, "If we can just get through Christmas . . ."?

On the day before Christmas, one family was at wits' end. The father and mother were frazzled from too much work and too many bills. They were on the verge of nervous breakdowns. Their young daughter felt like she was in the way. They had fussed at her and at each other all day long. We can almost understand why, with the frustrations of the day weighing down upon her, the little girl got her words mixed up in her bedtime prayer and said, "Give us this day our daily bread and forgive us our Christmases, as we forgive those who Christmas against us."

Christmas or confusion, Bethlehem or bedlam: Which will you choose this year? The truth is, we don't have to choose because Christmas always happens right in the midst of our confusion. God breaks into our confusion and becomes known through Jesus Christ. Christmas and confusion: Weren't they intimately related at the first Christmas when Jesus was born? Sometimes we forget that. However, this book is about how Christ breaks into our chaos and confusion to bring Christmas and how Bethlehem always happens in the midst of bedlam.

It is my hope and prayer that as we go through these pages (and the hectic days of Advent) together, we will find the freedom, the peace, the faith, the hope, and the love of Christmas and, in the midst of this year's hectic pace and boisterous bedlam, we will once again find the joy, the amazing grace, and the awesome miracle of Bethlehem.

1

Bethlehem or Bedlam

Scripture: Luke 2:8-14

A few years ago, I had the privilege of touring the Holy Land. It was a magnificent experience. What a thrill it was to see the Jordan River, the Sea of Galilee, the Mount of Olives, the Mount of Transfiguration, the ancient marketplace, the upper room, the Garden of Resurrection, the village of Jericho, and the Holy City of Jerusalem! Just being in those historic and sacred places was wonderfully mind-boggling to me. As we traveled back toward our hotel at the end of each day, tired but exhilarated, I found myself humming the song "I Walked Today Where Jesus Walked" and sensing something of the impact of what that songwriter must have felt when he first penned those words.

Early one morning, we started toward Bethlehem. *Bethlehem*. We were actually going to that sacred place where the Christ Child was born. I couldn't wait! Even though it was January, I was ready for Christmas in Bethlehem. As the tour bus slowed to enter the city, I glanced out the window; and I couldn't believe my eyes. On the Bethlehem hillside, there were some shepherds keeping watch over their flocks. It looked like a perfect scene for a Christmas card. I was touched and inspired by the simple, serene splendor of that sight.

However, when we arrived in the city, it was anything but serene splendor! It was a madhouse, total bedlam with loud music; gaudy signs; gross commercialism; merchants shouting and hawking their souvenirs like there was no tomorrow; people milling about, pushing, and shoving; poor children everywhere, begging for money; and our tour director warning us to watch out for pickpockets.

"Wait a minute!" I wanted to shout. "This is Bethlehem, not Bourbon Street! This is Bethlehem, not Times Square!" It was indeed Bethlehem, but it seemed more like Bedlam. I wanted Christmas, but it felt like confusion! My heart sank. I felt let down, disappointed, and disillusioned. As we walked into the Church of the Nativity and approached the spot built to honor Christ's birth, I was amazed to see that the same carnival-like atmosphere prevailed there as well. Even the chapel was loud, boisterous, commercial, and chaotic, with hucksters selling trinkets, T-shirts, pictures, and postcards. My spirit sagged even more. I wanted Bethlehem, but it was all bedlam.

Then something happened to change how I was feeling. A girl who looked to be six or seven years old was standing there with her mother, who was explaining to her that this was the place where Jesus was born on the first Christmas. Then, in the midst of the hucksters, merchants, and tourists, that girl did a beautiful thing. She dropped to her knees. Then she bowed her head and said, "Thank you, God, for sending Jesus! Amen."

As I heard the simple, sincere prayer of that little girl, it suddenly was Christmas in my heart! Once again, Christmas had come through a little child in Bethlehem. Bedlam had become Bethlehem. It was a touching moment, and it made me realize something: Christmas always happens right in the midst of our confusion. We don't have to choose between Bethlehem and Bedlam. They go together. They always have. That's the good news, isn't it? God breaks into our confusion, our bedlam and becomes known through Jesus Christ.

Bethlehem and bedlam: Weren't they intimately related at the first Christmas when Jesus was born? Sometimes we forget that. Remember the bedlam in Bethlehem that night? Just think of it—a crowded inn, a stable, a census, political intrigue, soldiers marching in the street, a busy city, people pushing and shoving, people scrambling for shelter. In that bedlam in Bethlehem so many centuries ago, Christmas happened. Christmas broke through! In that busy, hectic uproar, it happened; and those with the eyes, ears, and hearts of faith saw it, heard it, and felt it.

One year, I received a Christmas card from one of our church's college students. It had been mailed during her exam week, a busy, frantic time. On the back of the envelope, she had scribbled the following poem:

> I longed to be alone with God,
> to thank Him for His grace,
> and have a quiet peaceful talk,
> in some secluded place.
> But yet confronting me each day,
> were tasks I could not shirk;
> "You just go right ahead," said God,
> "We'll visit while we work!"

This is the good news of Christmas: God meets us where we are. God breaks into our uproar, our busyness, our hectic pace, our darkness, and our confusion through the birth of Jesus in Bethlehem—Jesus, who we know as the King of kings, the light of the world, and the gracious, forgiving One who understands.

I don't always identify with some of the popular songs of our time. However, every so often, I find one with a special message. A few years ago, Mac Davis wrote and recorded a song that haunted me. It is called "Every Now and Then," and the chorus reminds us that we can find comfort because every now and then something happens that is full of hope and wonder: "Every now and then, a blind squirrel finds an acorn/ Every now and then, a crippled sparrow takes to the wing."

Every now and then, we find Bethlehem. Every now and then, the real spirit, the real meaning of Christmas, breaks through the fog, the bedlam, and the confusion to clear up things. That's the experience that keeps us going.

We Find Bethlehem When We Discover Who God Is and What God Is Like

That is, the birth of Jesus in Bethlehem clears up the theological confusion. Christmas shows us what God is like. It gives us a new picture, and what it reveals is good news and glad tidings. I heard a story about a seven-year-old boy who had been playing outside. His mother called him in for dinner. The boy ran in, jumped into his chair, and grabbed his fork, ready to eat. "Wait, Tommy," said his mom, "you have germs on your hands. Gotta wash up before we eat." Tommy scrambled down, ran and washed his hands, came back, climbed into his chair, grabbed his fork, and started to eat. But again, his mother stopped him: "Wait, Tommy. We must say the blessing before we eat. We want to thank God for our food." Tommy put down his fork, mournfully shook his head, and muttered wearily, "Germs and God, germs and God, that's all I ever hear around here, and I haven't seen either one of them."

We can sympathize with Tommy's predicament, but Jesus' birth in Bethlehem does give God a face. Christmas shows us who God is and what God is like. William Barclay put it like this: "Jesus is the one person who can tell us what God is like and what God means us to be. In him alone, we see what God is and what we ought to be. Before Jesus came, people had only vague and shadowy, and often quite wrong, ideas about God; they could only at best guess and grope; but Jesus could say: 'Whoever has seen me has seen the Father' (John 14:9). In Jesus we see the love, the compassion, the mercy, the seeking heart and the purity of God as nowhere else in all this world. With the coming of Jesus, the time of guessing is gone and the time of certainty is come. . . . Jesus came to tell us the truth about God and the truth about ourselves."[1]

This, you see, is the good news of Christmas. Jesus shows us what God is like and the word is *love*. God is not an angry judge who must be appeased. God is not a powermonger demanding a "pound of flesh." Rather, God is like a loving parent who cares, who understands, and who is concerned about the welfare of God's children. Jesus said more than once, "Do not be afraid" and "Do not worry." It is also interesting to note that in the Christmas story in Luke's Gospel, the first thing the angel says to the shepherds is "Do not be afraid. . . . I am bringing you good news" (Luke 2:10). This is the most significant gift of Christmas.

In Jesus, God gives to us a new understanding of what God is like, a new experience of God's compassion and tenderness, a new relationship with God not built on fear but built on love. Every now and then, in the midst of bedlam, we find Bethlehem. We are reminded that God loves us, and that's the thing that keeps us going.

We Find Bethlehem When We Discover How to Relate to Other People

Every now and then, Christmas breaks through the fog and shows us that people are more important than objects and are not pawns to be used and manipulated. Persons are to be loved and appreciated. Jesus, who was born in Bethlehem, clears up the ethical confusion and reminds us to love our neighbors. Finding Bethlehem gives us a new respect and regard for others.

I remember a *Peanuts* cartoon I once saw. Charlie Brown and Linus are watching television. Snoopy, the dog, is standing on top of the TV set with his ears stuck up in a V shape. He is serving as the antenna. Then Charlie Brown says to Linus, "I don't understand it either. All I know is that he gives us a better picture." That could be said about Jesus, couldn't it? I am quick to confess that I don't understand everything about the coming of the Christ Child. All I know is that Jesus gives us a better picture. He sharpens the image. He clears up the confusion a bit and shows us not only what God is like but also what God wants us to be like. Jesus shows us dramatically that the best way to show our love for God is to love God's children.

Some years ago, a letter came to our home that moved me. It was from a friend named Wanda. Wanda had invited me to come to her church to speak at a special Christmas program early in December. Because of the hectic pace of the Christmas rush, I really didn't think I should go; but because of my appreciation for Wanda, I accepted and went. Two days later, the letter came to my house. It was a letter from Wanda, but the letter was not addressed to me. It was addressed to our children, Jodi and Jeff. They were six and nine years old at the time. Part of the letter read: "Dear Jodi and Jeff, I know most of the mail that comes to your house goes to your mom and dad, so I wanted to write to you. I am writing to thank you for sharing your dad with our community. You are so nice to share him with others, and I want you to know that I appreciate it."

When the children let me see the letter, my eyes filled with tears as I read it because I was so touched by her thoughtfulness, much more than I would have been if she had written me a letter. Then it broke through to me: That's what Christmas is really all about. Love for the children is the best way to show love for the Father. If you want to express your love and appreciation to God, then the best way to do it is to love God's children.

This is what the prophets meant when they said that God doesn't care about burnt offerings, sacrifices, or lavish prayers. What God really wants is for us to be merciful, kind, forgiving, thoughtful, and loving to one another. That's why Jesus Christ came—to show us how to care, to teach us how to love, and to remind us that we are family. We find Bethlehem once again when we practice such love toward one another.

We Find Bethlehem When We Discover What Really Matters

Finding Bethlehem clears up confusion about priorities. I once heard an old story about priorities. Jack Smith had been asked by his church to do one of the Christmas social-concerns projects. He was assigned the task of taking two boys from a low-income home on a

Christmas Eve shopping spree. Timmy, age nine, and his younger brother Billy, age seven, were delighted when Jack came from the church to pick them up. They had been watching for him all morning with great excitement because their dad was unemployed, and they knew this was all the Christmas they would get this year.

Jack gave each boy his allotted four dollars, and they started out together. Jack took them first to a toy store; but strangely, Timmy and Billy didn't seem to be interested. Jack made suggestions, but their answer was always a solemn, shake-of-the-head no.

Then, they tried a hobby shop but with the same results. Then they tried a candy store and a sporting goods store. They even tried a boys' clothing store but with no luck. Timmy and Billy would whisper to each other and look at a piece of brown wrapping paper stuck in a pocket, but nothing had struck their fancy yet. Finally, Jack asked, "Where would you boys like to look next?" Their faces brightened; this was the moment they had been waiting for. "Could we go to a shoe store, sir?" answered Timmy. "We really want to get a pair of shoes for our Daddy so he can go to work."

In the shoe store, the clerk asked what the boys wanted. Out came the brown paper. "We want a pair of work shoes to fit this foot," they said. Billy explained that it was the outline of their dad's foot, drawn with a crayon while their father was asleep in a chair. The clerk measured the outline of the foot and found some shoes that would fit. "Will these do?" he asked. The boys were delighted. Billy and Timmy, with big smiles, took the shoes into their hands eagerly. But then, Timmy saw the price: "Oh no, Billy. These shoes are $16.95, but we only have $8.00." The clerk, clearing his throat, said, "Well, that's the regular price, but you're in luck. It just so happens that those shoes are on sale today only for $5.98." With the shoes happily in hand, Timmy and Billy then bought gifts for their mother and two little sisters. Not once did they think of themselves.

The day after Christmas, Jack saw the boys' father out on the street looking for a job. He had the new shoes on his feet and gratitude in his eyes. He said to Jack, "I thank God for people like you who care." Jack answered, "Thank God for your two sons. They taught me more about Christmas in one day than I had learned in a lifetime."

[1] From *The Gospel of Matthew, Volume 1*, Revised Updated Edition, by William Barclay (Westminster John Knox Press, 2001), pages 24-25.

Questions for Reflection and Discussion

1. What is the Christmas season like for you? When has the season felt more like bedlam than a celebration of Jesus' birth in Bethlehem?

2. What images, thoughts, or feelings come to you when you think about Bethlehem? When have you discovered Bethlehem in the midst of bedlam?

3. What questions do you have about what God is like? How does Jesus help you answer those questions?

4. When have you experienced bedlam in your relationships with others? with family? with friends? with strangers? What hope does Jesus offer for times of bedlam in your relationships?

5. What does the story about Billy and Timmy say to you about priorities? How does Jesus help you rediscover what is most important in your life?

Prayer

God, you offer yourself to us in all of life, even in the bedlam, confusion, and chaos that often surrounds us. Thank you. Help us to find Bethlehem, to see Jesus, and to trust that you are with us. In Christ we pray. Amen.

Focus for the Week

Finding Bethlehem means discovering the good news that in the birth of Jesus Christ, God meets us where we are, even in the midst of bedlam. Each day this week, identify one way you experience the love and support of God as you look forward to celebrating the birth of Jesus Christ. Offer a daily prayer of gratitude for God's presence in all areas of life.

Daily Devotions

Read the Scriptures for the daily devotions and reflect on what they say to you about finding God in the midst of life's bedlam. Consider how the Scriptures offer hope as you look forward to celebrating the birth of Jesus. Record your insights in the space provided.

Day One
Isaiah 7:10-17

The Sign of Immanuel

The people of Judah, the Southern Kingdom, lived under the threat of an invasion by the superpower Assyria that utterly destroyed the Northern Kingdom in 722 B.C. The prophet Isaiah addresses the pending bedlam by advising King Ahaz not to enter into alliances with foreign powers but to rely on God alone.

Isaiah gives Ahaz the sign of Immanuel, which means "God With Us," prophesying that a woman will give birth to a child and will call him Immanuel. He says that by the time the child is old enough "to refuse the evil and choose the good" (verse 16), Assyria will no longer be a threat to Judah and Jerusalem.

Though the sign of Immanuel addresses the Assyrian threat to Judah, Christians find hope and meaning in this Scripture passage as a prophecy of God's presence in the birth of Jesus. Matthew 1:23 quotes Isaiah 7:14 and uses the prophecy to refer to Jesus. It is Jesus rather than the Roman emperor who embodies God's saving presence. The biblical witness is consistent: God is with us, even in the midst of bedlam.

How does the name Immanuel speak to you about God's presence?

In what ways have you experienced Immanuel, or "God With Us," during times of bedlam or confusion?

Day Two
Isaiah 9:6-7

A Just and Righteous King

The prophet Isaiah proclaimed God's power and dominion over all nations. He understood that God chose the king and favored him for all eternity. Even though Jerusalem and the king may suffer, God would never let the city be destroyed and King David's dynasty would never fall. The bedlam of the Syro-Ephraimitic war and the threat of Assyrian domination would not shake Isaiah's faith nor change his exalted views of God and of God's chosen city.

Isaiah 9 describes a vision of an ideal messianic king who would establish endless peace and uphold the reign forever with justice and righteousness (verse 7). Isaiah describes this king with the names: "Wonderful Counselor, Mighty God, Everlasting Father, Prince of Peace" (verse 6). In Christian tradition, Isaiah's names for the ideal king of Jerusalem have become beloved names for Jesus.

Which of the names for Isaiah's ideal king do you like best? Why? What do the names say to you about Jesus?

What names would you give to Jesus? Why?

Day Three
Isaiah 11:1-9

A Peaceful Kingdom

As in Isaiah 9:6-7, the theme of Isaiah 11:1-9 tells about Isaiah's vision of the ideal king of Jerusalem who is chosen and favored by God. This king is the shoot from the stump of Jesse, David's father. The "spirit of the LORD" (verse 2) will be with this king, and he will reign with righteousness and faithfulness. He will be concerned for those who are poor and marginalized (verse 4). The society will be blessed with peace and harmony that will spread throughout all nature. It will be a world without predators and victims, a world in which "the earth will be full of the knowledge of the LORD" (verse 9).

Christians see the ideal king fulfilled in Jesus and believe that in God's fullness of time, Jesus will reign over an eternally peaceful realm based on God's ways of justice and righteousness. Even in the bedlam and messiness of contemporary political conflicts and ongoing disregard for the poor and the marginalized in our world, we have faith in God's steadfast love and presence in Jesus Christ. In Jesus, we find hope for the ultimate transformation of our world into God's peaceful kingdom.

What inspires or challenges you about Isaiah's vision of
the ideal king? of the peaceful Kingdom?

How do you see Isaiah's vision fulfilled in Jesus Christ?

Day Four
Jeremiah 31:31-34

A New Covenant

Another time of intense bedlam in the lives of the people of Judah was the Babylonian invasion. Babylon destroyed Jerusalem and the Temple in 587 B.C.; and in 597 B.C. and in 587 B.C., many of its leaders and citizens were exiled in Babylon. In spite of this bedlam, Jeremiah 31:31-34 offers words of comfort and hope in the promise of a restored relationship with God. Even though the people had broken the covenant given to them at Mount Sinai (Exodus 19–20), God will enter into a stronger relationship in which the law will be written on their hearts.

While the prophet is speaking of God's relationship with the house of Israel (verse 33), Christians understand faith in Jesus Christ as a continuation of God's covenant and as confirmation that God is always with us. God does not break or discard God's covenant promises. We do. Much of our bedlam and confusion occurs when we stray from God's love and from God's ways of mercy and justice. God writes on our hearts God's love, God's ways, and God's forgiveness. In Jesus Christ, we can find peace and strength in the promise that God will never abandon us.

When have you strayed from your relationship with God and from living according to God's ways? What was it like?

How might you open your heart to a restored relationship
with God through Jesus Christ? What might be different
for you?

Day Five
John 14:7-11

Seeing God in Jesus

Before the bedlam and confusion of Jesus' arrest, trial, and crucifixion, Jesus offers words of hope and assurance to his disciples. Jesus explains to them that his presence in the world and all that he says and does reveals the Father to them. The disciples, especially Philip, have difficulty understanding him. Philip says, "Lord, show us the Father, and we will be satisfied" (verse 8). In response, Jesus says to him, "Whoever has seen me has seen the Father" (verse 9). Jesus encourages the disciples to believe that he is in the Father and that the Father is in him. He recognizes the difficulty they have with accepting this reality: "If you do not, then believe me because of the works themselves" (verse 11).

No matter what bedlam lies ahead for us as contemporary followers of Jesus, we too can find hope and assurance in him as the incarnate Word of God. In Jesus, God is with us. In Jesus, we can see God.

What challenges you or inspires you about Jesus' assertion
that those who see him see the Father? What does this
assertion mean to you?

How does Jesus help you see God? What does he reveal to you about God's nature?

Day Six
Colossians 1:15-20

The Fullness of God

The opening thanksgiving section of the letter to the followers of Christ at Colossae contains a majestic hymn about the presence and activity of God in Jesus Christ. It echoes the themes of creation and incarnation that we read about in the Gospel of John (1:1-3, 14-18). If God were visible, God would look like Christ. Christ existed outside the confines of time before the world was created. All things were created through Christ. Everything holds together in Christ. God's intent through Christ is to bring all creation back into harmony with God. The cosmic scope of this hymn is almost beyond human comprehension! It sets the stage for the main concern of the letter, addressing philosophies that threatened the faith of the Colossian Christians (2:8-9).

The letter presents Christ as the One in whom they have unity. As the body of believers, they are encouraged to "hold fast to the head, from whom the whole body, nourished and held together by its ligaments and sinews, grows with a growth that is from God" (2:19).

When we begin to comprehend that the fullness of God as Creator and Redeemer of all creation is in Christ and that Christ is the One who binds us together, we discover the wonder and joy of the birth in Bethlehem: "For in him all the fullness of God was pleased to dwell" (1:19).

How does this hymn in Colossians inspire you? How does it challenge you? What does it say to you about God's relationship to human beings?

How do you see the fullness of God in Christ? How
does seeing the fullness of God in Christ help you find
Bethlehem in the midst of bedlam?

2

Christ Came to
Set Us Free

Scripture: Galatians 5:13-15

L et me begin with a parable, the Parable of
the Locksmith.[1]
Once upon a time, there were some
slaves in prison. They had been slaves in
that prison for so long that they had forgotten they were
slaves and were in prison. In fact, they decided that they
were free and that the walls surrounding them did not
imprison them at all, but rather imprisoned the people
outside. The prisoners could often hear cries of pain from
the other side of the wall. Once, a few of the prisoners
escaped, but they came back. They told of wandering
in the wilderness for years, of having to fight for their
homes, of the problems of government, of the cruelty of
war, and of other ongoing anxieties outside. They came
back to the prison, back to the calm, secure, unchanging,
less-threatening prison. Life is easier in here, they

thought; and since prison is supposed to make life harder, they decided that they must not be in prison. They said over and over to themselves that the people outside were the prisoners: "They are the prisoners! Not us!"

The prisoners went right on dreaming that they were free. Of course, their existence was not always peaceful and quiet. One day, a young locksmith came in over the wall. He not only told the prisoners that they were slaves and in prison, but he also did something much worse. He broke the locks on the prison door! With the door unlocked and pushed open, the cries of need and pain from outside the wall were no longer muffled; they rang out louder and louder and louder. Then the young locksmith had the audacity to tell the inmates that now they were free and should live outside the prison. He told them to "go out into all the world!"

A few of the prisoners believed him, but most of them said he was a troublemaker. They thought that anyone could plainly see that true happiness was right there where they were. The prisoners decided that this locksmith was a social menace; and for the good of the community, he ought to be silenced and done away with before he ruined things. So, they had a quick trial and accused him of being a dangerous troublemaker who was upsetting people and disturbing the peace. He was declared guilty and executed for the good of the community, they said piously. And then they said, "There! That takes care of that."

The locksmith's followers had been afraid and quiet during the trial and execution. But when they discovered that the doors could never be locked again, they began spreading the locksmith's message. Many of them were killed as well; but their companions kept on working, serving, and preaching. Every now and then, some folks believed the locksmith's message. They accepted the fact that they were in slavery. They recognized that they were indeed in prison. And they went out the unlocked door to freedom, entering the world of pain, need, and service.

However, many of the inmates kept on dreaming that they were free. They never looked out the door for fear they might see someone in need, someone in trouble, or some problem that needed solving. They didn't want to see anything like that. They put cotton in their ears to muffle the noise of cries for help. They didn't want to hear anything like that. They continued to believe that it was the people on the other side of the wall who were imprisoned, not them. They could not understand why the young locksmith broke the locks on the prison doors.

This parable strikes me. It is an unusual and relevant parable for us today because all around us, most everywhere we look, people are still in prison. People are still slaves to selfishness and pride, still imprisoned by hatred and jealousy, still bound by complacency and apathy and closed-mindedness. People still misunderstand the meaning of freedom, salvation, and deliverance. But the good news of the parable is that Jesus Christ is the locksmith.

Jesus Christ, who was born in Bethlehem, is the one who breaks the locks and throws open the prison door! He sends us out into the world. He calls us to be not just human but humane. He saves us not just *from* something but also *for* something! He breaks the locks on the prison door and sends us out into the needy, hurting world so that we might be instruments of love, peace, reconciliation, forgiveness, and compassion. He gives his life for us so that we might give our lives for others. We are set free to be servants.

That's what Paul is talking about in Galatians 5. Remember how he put it in these verses: "For you were called to freedom, . . . only do not use your freedom as an opportunity for self-indulgence, but through love become slaves to one another. For the whole law is summed up in a single commandment, 'You shall love your neighbor as yourself'" (verses 13-14).

In the Parable of the Locksmith, Christ is portrayed as a troublemaker. This is unusual for us because most often we think of Christ as the comforter who brings healing and speaks peace to troubled hearts. This is well and good, but we also need to remember that Isaiah said the Messiah will "startle many nations" (52:15). And as a matter of fact, Christ did disturb people. Go, read the New Testament! Christ troubled Herod and Rome. He disturbed Pilate, religious leaders, and even his own disciples. In the New Testament, the Christ who comforts broken hearts is also the one who disturbs complacent people and exposes hypocrisy, self-centeredness, and superficiality. Here in this parable, Christ the Locksmith is seen as one who disturbs us, startles us, shakes us out of our prisons, and sends us out into all the world to be servants. Now, what are some of the prisons that threaten us today? There are many. Let me list just a few, and I'm sure you will think of others.

Christ Frees Us From the Prison of Selfishness

One of the dramatic things the Christian faith says to us is that selfishness won't work. Selfishness doesn't fill the emptiness within. It's an empty shell. It's a dark and debilitating prison. Christ comes to say, "Get out of that prison! Come out into the world of love and caring and sharing."

Jesus' teachings about the dangers of selfishness are almost startling. Empty your mind for a moment and listen to these words of Jesus as if you were hearing them for the first time:

"If any want to become my followers, let them deny themselves and take up their cross and follow me. For those who want to save their life will lose it, and those who lose their life for my sake will find it. For what will it profit them if they gain the whole world but forfeit their life?" (Matthew 16:24-26).

"I give you a new commandment, that you love one another. Just as I have loved you, you also should love one another" (John 13:34).

Do you understand what Jesus is saying? He is saying, "Get out of the prison of selfishness. The doors are open now. The locks are broken. Come on out into the world of love and compassion."

Saint Francis of Assisi (Italy, 13th century) shows us in his magnificent prayer what it means to be set free

by Christ, what it means to be set free from selfishness.
You've seen it in print. You've prayed it aloud. You've
heard it sung. Now look closely again at these words:

> Lord, make me an instrument of thy peace;
> where there is hatred, let me sow love;
> where there is injury, pardon;
> where there is doubt, faith;
> where there is despair, hope;
> where there is darkness, light;
> and where there is sadness, joy.
>
> O Divine Master,
> grant that I may not so much seek
> to be consoled as to console;
> to be understood, as to understand;
> to be loved, as to love;
> for it is in giving that we receive,
> it is in pardoning that we are pardoned,
> and it is in dying that we are born to eternal life.

Christ breaks the locks on the prison of selfishness, but we
have to decide to walk out the door.

Christ Frees Us From the Prison of Hate

The Christian faith teaches that hatred won't work.
Jesus knew that hating others is not only hurtful to them,
but also can destroy our souls. Hate is a terrible prison.

I once heard an ancient Greek legend that shows us the danger of hate. According to the legend, two Greek athletes were close friends. They were like brothers. But then, one of them began to receive more recognition, even to the point where the townspeople built a statue of him to honor him as their number-one athlete. The other man became jealous and hateful. Every night after dark, he would go out and try to destroy the statue. Finally, he succeeded. He toppled the heavy statue off its pedestal, but it fell on him and crushed him to death! He was destroyed by his bitterness, crushed by his own hate.

That's the way hate works. It turns on us. It boomerangs. It comes back to haunt us. It is so destructive. Jesus knew that; and he preached love, compassion, and kindness. He exposed hate as a terrible and malignant enemy. Christ breaks the locks on the prisons of selfishness and hate, but we have to decide to walk out the door.

Christ Frees Us From the Prison of Unconcern

Christ came into the world to show us how concerned God is, how much God cares, how deeply God loves; and he sends us out into the world so that we may love and care for people in the same self-giving way.

A few years ago, I saw something that fascinated me. I had walked to the burger joint just down Westheimer Road to pick up a quick lunch. After I placed my takeout order, I noticed a middle-aged woman sitting alone in a booth by the window, eating a hamburger and fries with a large chocolate milkshake. She was a muscular, commanding, powerful-looking woman who gave the distinct impression that she could be a drill sergeant at Paris Island or play offensive guard for the Houston Texans. All of a sudden, she glanced out the window. "Oh my goodness," she said, "look at those kids!" I looked and saw three small children. They were in their swimsuits, with towels draped over their shoulders. They had evidently been swimming, and now they were trying to get back across Westheimer Road.

The three children were holding hands, and they were leaning forward like they were about to run a race. They were watching for an opportunity to dash across the busiest street in the city! At that moment, it seemed even busier than usual. Suddenly, the woman who looked like a drill sergeant barked at me: "You! Watch my food!" And I said what anyone in his or her right mind would have said at that moment: "Yes, ma'am!" She bolted out of the restaurant, rushed to the children, and signaled them to wait. Then, with the authority of a seasoned and confident traffic cop, she marched out into the middle of Westheimer, held up her powerful arm, and stopped all four lanes of traffic. Then she went back to the children, took them by the hand, and walked them across the street as bewildered but obedient motorists watched with some amusement and much appreciation. When she had escorted the children safely across the busy street, she strode back across and then motioned the traffic back to life.

Now, let me ask you something: What was it that gave that woman the courage, the strength, and the guts to do that? The answer is simple: It was love! As she returned to her food I had been dutifully guarding, I said to her, "That was a nice thing you did." She said, "Well, I love kids, and that was a dangerous situation. They needed help. Somebody needed to do something to help them. And since I'm a Christian, it became my responsibility." The point is obvious: Love is so powerful that it can even stop the traffic on Westheimer. And that's saying something! When you are a Christian, love is your responsibility.

As I thought about that special act of love, I realized her action is precisely the kind of concern we are supposed to have for all of God's children. Christ came to break the locks on the prisons of selfishness, hate, and unconcern. He came to set us free, but we have to decide to walk out the door.

[1] Featured in Dr. Moore's book *Daddy, Is That Story True, or Were You Just Preaching?* (Abingdon Press, 2012); available at *cokesbury.com*.

Questions for Reflection and Discussion

1. What thoughts or feelings do you have about the parable at the beginning of this chapter? What are the safe places in your life?

2. When do you think a safe place can be a prison?

3. How might the safe places in your life function more like prisons that prevent you from fulfilling your God-given potential as a follower of Christ?

4. How do you respond to the naming of selfishness, hate, and unconcern as prisons? What other prisons do you think threaten our full potential?

5. When have you felt a need to reach out to others or to try something new in your life?

6. How might you find Bethlehem within and outside the safe places in your life?

Prayer

God of life and hope, we thank you for the gift of freedom in Jesus Christ. Help us to claim it every day so that others may find Bethlehem and realize they are also free from the prisons of their lives. In Christ we pray. Amen.

Focus for the Week

We find Bethlehem when we discover and claim the freedom given to us through Jesus Christ. This week, consider how you can "step out the door" in service to God and others. Think about ways this step might enrich your life and help you grow in faith.

Daily Devotions

Read the Scriptures for the daily devotions and reflect on what they say to you about discovering and claiming the freedom God gives to us through Christ. In what ways can you use your freedom to serve others? Record your insights in the space provided.

Day One
Luke 4:16-19

The Mission of Jesus

In Luke's Gospel, Jesus, the One born in Bethlehem, initiates his public ministry by reading from the Scroll of Isaiah. He describes his mission by referring to Isaiah's words of hope for the restoration of Israel (see Isaiah 58:6; 61:1-2). It is a mission that is empowered by God's Spirit and that resonates with the good news of release, recovery, and freedom. Release, recovery, and freedom suggest a return to human wholeness and a restored relationship with God. As Jesus reads in the synagogue, we hear echoes of the promise and hope expressed within Mary's song of praise in Luke 1:46-56. God is merciful and remembers the lowly and the needy (verses 52-53).

Jesus' concern is also for those who are poor, who are captives, who are blind, and who are oppressed. These include any who are socially or religiously marginalized by economic hardship, by gender, by illness, or by anything that prevents them from knowing wholeness and freedom in relationship with others and with God. We can hear and respond to them, especially as we anticipate the celebration of his birth in Bethlehem. We can ask ourselves, *What holds us captive? What makes us blind? What oppresses us?* We can be assured that freedom is ours in Christ. When we claim and proclaim the freedom Christ offers, we find Bethlehem.

What good news do you need to hear in these hectic days before Christmas? How do you understand the gift of freedom in Christ?

How does Jesus' reading from Isaiah address your need for wholeness and a restored relationship with God?

Day Two
Luke 13:10-17

You Are Set Free

Luke 13:10-17 describes the healing of a woman; however, the story is much more than a simple healing narrative. It contains a challenge to a leader of the synagogue to prioritize human need over and above regulations for religious life. The woman has suffered an ailment that has kept her in a bent-over position for eighteen years. She does not ask to be healed. Jesus sees her; and even though it is the sabbath, he tells her, "Woman, you are set free from your ailment." He lays hands on her and heals her. She stands up straight and praises God.

The synagogue leader, rather than rejoicing for the restoration of wholeness and dignity to the woman, chastises Jesus for doing the work of healing on the sabbath. Jesus answers the leader with a graphic challenge. On the sabbath, any of those present would untie their oxen and donkeys from the feeding trough in order to take them to drink water. The woman, a daughter of Abraham, deserves to be set free, to be shown the same care and compassion as is shown to the animals. His statement to the crowd restores dignity to the woman, just as the healing restored her to wholeness and led her to praise God. It reminds all of us that we can be bound up and that we may need to be set free from attitudes that prevent us from showing compassion to others.

What situations in your life keep you bound up or bent over?

_____

_____

_____

_____

_____

_____

_____

_____

_____

_____

_____

_____

_____

_____

_____

_____

_____

_____

_____

_____

_____

_____

_____

_____

_____

_____

_____

_____

What would it be like to hear for yourself the words, "You are set free"?

Day Three
John 8:28-32

The Truth Will Set You Free

What truth is Jesus talking about? What must we know or do to experience freedom? Jesus is referring to the presence of God (verses 27-29)! As he addresses believers, he centers that truth in his word. If they continue in their relationship with his word, they will know the truth. *Word*, or *logos* in Greek, evokes the creative word of God that began the Gospel of John (1:1-3) as well as the teachings of Jesus.

To be Jesus' disciple and to stay attuned to Jesus' word makes it possible to know the truth of God's presence in Jesus Christ. This truth sets us free. It is what we celebrate at the birth of Jesus in Bethlehem. When we celebrate knowing that God is with us in Jesus Christ and claim for ourselves the freedom we find in that truth, we find Bethlehem.

Read verse 31. What does it mean to you to continue in Jesus' word?

Read verse 32. What feelings or thoughts do you have about this verse? What does it mean to know that the truth will set you free?

Day Four
Romans 8:1-6

Free From Sin and Death

Using language that evokes the memory of God's gift of freedom as seen in the story of the Exodus from Egypt, Paul talks about God's saving action through Jesus Christ as the gift that offers freedom through life in the Spirit.

The conversation is imbedded in his understanding of the law. Paul has great respect for the law as just, holy, and good (Romans 7:12). God's work in Jesus does not undo the gift of the law. It is the presence of God's Spirit of life in Jesus Christ that makes it possible for us to live according to God's law. Paul reminds us that our tendency to live according to the flesh interferes with our ability to live God's way. Living according to the flesh means living according to rebellious and corruptible human nature in our physical lives.

God offers the Spirit of life in Jesus Christ, which "sets us free" from the sin and death of living in the flesh. Sin is a corruptible and destructive force capable of dwelling within us and causing death. In Jesus Christ, we are "set free" to live according to the ways of the indwelling Spirit of God. Paul understands that we are free to set our minds on the Spirit. He reminds us, "To set the mind on the flesh is death, but to set the mind on the Spirit is life and peace" (verse 6).

How do you respond to the idea that human nature is
rebellious and corruptible? Do you agree or disagree?
Why?

What does it mean to you to set your mind on the Spirit?
How can setting your mind on the Spirit of life in Jesus
Christ make a difference in your life from day to day?
How does this choice set you free?

Day Five
Romans 8:18-25

Creation Will Be Set Free

Romans 8:18-25 presses beyond the boundaries of human freedom to the freedom given to all creation! The passage expands and explains this freedom in the context of suffering: "The sufferings of this present time are not worth comparing with the glory about to be revealed to us" (verse 18). Paul then leaps into the more cosmic scale of God's redemption. The creation waits for God's glory to be revealed in God's children. We hear echoes of God's original intent for creation as described in Genesis. God's human children were intended to be stewards of creation, but their disobedience caused the creation itself to be cursed (Genesis 3:17-18). Creation suffers along with and because of humans, and God's intent is to sustain and redeem humans and all creation.

Isaiah promises a new heaven and a new earth (65:17-25; 66:22). When God's redeeming work, begun in Jesus Christ, finds completion in the age to come, humans and all creation will be set free.

What thoughts or feelings occur to you as you read Paul's understanding that all creation will be set free? What do you think will be different in creation when God's redeeming work finds completion?

In what ways can you participate now in God's ongoing redemption of all creation?

Day Six
2 Corinthians 3:17-18

The Lord's Spirit Gives Freedom

In 2 Corinthians 3, Paul tries to help the believers in Corinth grasp both his and their identity as followers of Jesus Christ. As in Romans 8, he reminds them that they are empowered by God's Spirit, the Spirit that dwells within them as individuals and as a body of believers. His beginning place is God's Spirit: "Now the Lord is the Spirit, and where the Spirit of the Lord is, there is freedom" (verse 17). He weaves together the ancient language of covenant and of God's glory through the gift of the Spirit given in Jesus Christ.

Christ, like a mirror, reflects God's glory. Believers who look at God's glory in Jesus experience transformation into the image of God, which recalls the Creation account in Genesis 1:27. Ongoing transformation marks the life of faith. Believers are works in progress, empowered by God's Spirit to become more Christlike and more identified with the glory of God. Believers have received God's Spirit through Christ. Along with Paul, they are part of the new covenant of God's Spirit, who gives the gift of freedom. This freedom means that believers are empowered to live according to God's holy, just, and righteous ways.

What does it mean to you that God's Spirit lives within and among believers? that believers are works in progress?

How do you understand the gift of freedom given by
God's Spirit? How does this gift inspire or challenge you?

3

Love Came Down in Bethlehem

Scripture: Matthew 11:1-6

My brother Bob is a minister in Tennessee. Because of the geographical distance between Texas and Tennessee and the demands of our careers, we don't get to be together as often as we would like. So, we try to make up for that by using the telephone. Our telephone visits are usually pretty much the same every time. We talk about family and the church, about current events and our reading lists. We talk about sports and the weather, and then usually our conversations turn to preaching. One conversation went like this: "What are you preaching about this Sunday?" Bob asked me. I answered, "Love Came Down at Christmas." "Hey! Wait a minute," he said. "I ran across a great quote recently that might be helpful if I can find it."

Well, he found it, and he was right. It is a powerful quote about love attributed to the noted French paleontologist and priest Pierre Teilhard de Chardin: "Someday, after mastering the winds, the waves, the tides and gravity, we shall harness for God the energies of love, and then, for a second time in the history of the world, man will have discovered fire."

We are a people who live in a time almost totally dedicated to the concept of power, especially to run all our machines, from cars to computers. We love power. Dr. D. L. Dykes put it like this: "We even want our detergents to have 'bulldozer power.' We want automobiles with 400-horsepower engines, capable of cruising at 120 miles an hour, when we know we have to drive in zones from 35 to 65 miles an hour. For the most part, our greatest sense of security is in believing that we are the strongest nation in the world . . . and we can sleep peacefully at night because of that sense of security. Power is a watchword of our time."[1] We are obsessed with power.

But let me ask you something: What is the most powerful force in the world? What is the strongest force on earth? Is it military might? Is it political clout or oratory? Is it influence or money or position? How would you answer that question? What is the most powerful force in the world? The Bible says it's love. In our modern world, we give so much time, energy, and effort chasing after the wrong kinds of power; and then along comes Christmas. We find Bethlehem, which calls us back to the power of love.

That's what this story in Matthew 11 is all about. While he is in prison, John the Baptist begins to get impatient with Jesus. They are cousins; they grew up together. Cooling his heels in prison, John gets antsy and sends his disciples out to Jesus with this question: "Are you the one who is to come, or are we to wait for another?" (verse 3). What John means is this: What are you waiting for? You have the power. When are you going to lead the march on Rome? When are you going to get with the program? When are you going to get this Kingdom going? When are you going to defeat the Romans and seize the throne?

But look at how Jesus answers: "Go and tell John what you hear and see: the blind receive their sight, the lame walk, the lepers are cleansed, the deaf hear, the dead are raised, and the poor have good news brought to them" (verses 4-5). Now, what did Jesus mean by that? Jesus meant that he had not chosen the way of might or power or wrath, but the way of love. He had chosen to bring the Kingdom with love because he knew that love is the most powerful force in the world. Let's break this down a bit and be more specific.

Love Is More Powerful Than Fame

The world teaches us that we can find power in position and fame, and the teaching is true to a degree. The problem is, the power associated with position and fame is so fleeting. It doesn't last. It fades and shrivels and dies. Ask Muhammad Ali. You know Ali, the unprecedented three-time world heavyweight boxing champion. At one time, he was considered to be the most famous person in the world. His face was always showing up on the covers of magazines and in newspapers. When he was "floating like a butterfly and stinging like a bee," he was king of his profession. Everywhere he went, he was trailed by an adoring entourage of reporters, trainers, support staff, and fans. But that was then. Where has Muhammad Ali been since those days of boxing fame? In 1988, seven years after losing his heavyweight title to Trevor Berbick, sportswriter Gary Smith went to find out.

Ali escorted Smith to a barn on his farmland. On the floor, leaning against the walls, were mementoes of Ali in his prime. Photos and portraits of the champ punching and dancing. Sculpted body. Fists flashing. Muscles rippling. Championship belt held high in triumph. The picture of power. But, the pictures in that barn were covered with layers of dust and cobwebs and evidence of the pigeons who had made his barn their home. Then, Ali did something significant. Perhaps it was a gesture of closure. Maybe it was a statement of despair. Whatever the reason, he walked over to the row of pictures and turned them, one by one, toward the wall. He then walked to the door, stared at the countryside, and mumbled something so low that Smith had to ask him to repeat it. Ali did. "I had the world," he said, "and it wasn't nothin'. Look now. . . ."[2]

Muhammad Ali was, without question, one of the greatest athletes this world has ever known. Today, he is a respected philanthropist. In spite of the progression of Parkinson's disease, he has traveled to many countries to help those in need; and in 1998, he was chosen to be a United Nations Messenger of Peace. He was awarded the Presidential Medal of Freedom in 2005. The same year, he opened the Muhammad Ali Center in his hometown of Louisville, Kentucky, which focuses on six core principles: confidence, conviction, dedication, giving, respect, and spirituality. He said, "I wanted a place that would inspire people to be the best that they could be at whatever they chose to do, and to encourage them to be respectful of one another."[3] Ali's words demonstrate a shift in power, a shift from the power of fame to the power of love. They remind us of the same thing that we learn from God's gift at Bethlehem. Love is more powerful than fame. Love is more important than fame. Love is more lasting than fame.

Love Is More Powerful Than Force

Many times in life, we believe that the best way to get something done is by force. For example, suppose that you have a child, and your control over that child is based on force. Your control over that child will last only as long as the child is at home with you where you can monitor behavior and the child is physically small enough for you to control. When the child is old enough to move away to a dormitory or into an apartment or is simply big enough to tell you "No," then you don't have any control over your child if the control has been based on force. However, if your relationship with the child is based on love, your relationship will be just the same as it was when he or she was a little child sitting at the dinner table at home, no matter where the child goes.

Who are the people who have the greatest control over us or influence on us? They are not the ones who threaten us with force. In fact, most of us tend to want to do the opposite when folk threaten us. The persons who have the most power over us are the ones who love us because love is stronger than force.

In the early days, before the time of Moses, people lived by "the law of the jungle," "survival of the fittest," and the spirit of force and revenge. "If you steal my ox, then I will plunder your village and destroy everything in sight. If you break my finger, I will break your arm and both legs. I will get you back and then some!"

But then along came Moses; and he took us a step forward by introducing God's law, which set limits on revenge. "Don't do anymore to them than they did to you. . . . If someone breaks the little finger of your left hand then you should do no more than break the little finger on their left hand. . . . If someone steals your ox, do no more than take one of their oxen. . . . An eye for an eye and a tooth for a tooth!" This represented an amazing progression in the civilizing process.

Then along came Jesus, who reintroduced the power of love in a fresh new way. He said an amazing thing that echoed the heartbeat of God's law: To love God and neighbor (Deuteronomy 6:5; Leviticus 19:18). In essence, he said, "You don't have to get them back. You don't have to exact revenge or retribution. You can forgive. You can reconcile. You can love!" In words and actions, over and over, this is what Jesus taught us: Love is the most beautiful and the most powerful thing in the world. And this is our calling as Christians: to take up the torch of Christ's redemptive love and carry it strongly into the future.

If you were to ask me to name my favorite Bible passage, one of the first passages that would come into my mind would be John 13:34-35. Jesus is in the upper room with his disciples, giving them their final instructions before he goes to the cross; and he says to them (and us) these incredible words: "I give you a new commandment, that you love one another. Just as I have loved you, you also should love one another. By this everyone will know that you are my disciples, if you have love for one another." I love these words from our Lord because they remind us that the most genuine, authentic sign of discipleship is love; and they remind us that Jesus is not just calling us to love, he is calling us to "Christlike love." The key phrases in this passage are "as I have loved you" and "love one another as I have loved you!" This is serious business here. Jesus wants us to imitate his loving spirit, to love as he loved—graciously, generously, sacrificially, and unconditionally. That kind of love can turn the world upside down, or better put, right side up, because that kind of Christlike love (as we learned at Golgotha) is the most beautiful and most powerful force in the world. That kind of love cannot be defeated, cannot be silenced, cannot be buried in a tomb. It resurrects! It always resurrects!

So, if you want to know what God is like and what God wants us to be like, remember Jesus. If you want to know the greatest power this world has ever seen, remember Jesus. Leaders will come and go, fads will flourish and fade, military establishments will rise and fall; but God's truth and love will keep marching on because love is more powerful than fame or force.

Love Is More Powerful Than Money

In our world today, we tend to believe that if we have enough money then we can do anything. "Money is power," we think.

One night, several years ago, I was called to the emergency room at a local hospital. A young man in our church had been involved in a horrible automobile accident in his sports car, and he was critically injured. He was still alive when I got there, but it was a grave situation.

I was standing beside the father, a wealthy and powerful man in the community, when the doctor came out and told him that they had done all they could do, but his son was going to die. The man grabbed the front of the doctor's surgical coat with one hand and with the other, he pulled out his billfold. He said, "Doctor, I am extremely wealthy. I have enough money to do anything for you or to bring any doctor or surgeon in the world here to save my son." Even as he spoke those words, though, I could see the expression on his face change. He realized that there are some things you can't buy, no matter how much money you have.

In 1907, the famous author Rudyard Kipling, spoke to the graduating class at McGill University in Montreal. He advised the graduates to not value too highly the prizes of power and wealth which this world offers. The following paraphrase comes from part of his famous speech: "Because someday you will meet someone who cares for none of these things and then if that is all you possess, you will know how poor you really are."

Jesus said, "Go and tell John what you hear and see: the blind receive their sight, the lame walk, the lepers are cleansed, the deaf hear, the dead are raised, and the poor have good news brought to them" (Matthew 11:4-5). This is the good news of Christmas, isn't it? Christ came to us in this world in the power of love. The Word of God became flesh and blood. The Word of God was wrapped up in a person named Jesus, who came and dwelt among us full of grace, full of truth, full of love. He could have chosen the way of might or clout or fame or wealth or force; but instead, he chose the way of love. He came as a Suffering Servant and a sacrificial Savior. He came to live in love that we might live meaningfully. He came to die in love that we might live eternally. In a very special way, "Love came down at Christmas, / Love all lovely, Love divine."[4]

[1] From *The Power of Love* by Dr. D.L. Dykes, Jr. (Abingdon Press, 1988) page 13.

[2] From "Ali And His Entourage" in *Sports Illustrated*, by Gary Smith (April 25, 1988); pages 48, 51.

[3] "Muhammad Ali," The Biography Channel website, http://www.biography.com/people/muhammad-ali-9181165 (accessed Jun 06, 2013).

[4] From "Love Came Down at Christmas," Words by Christina G. Rossetti, 1885.

Questions for Reflection and Discussion

1. What inspires or challenges you about the quote by Pierre Tielhard de Chardin (see page 72)?

2. How do you respond to the view that we love power and are "totally dedicated to the concept of power, especially to run all our machines, from cars to computers"? What kinds of power do you see at work in our culture?

3. Read Matthew 11:1-6 and the words to the hymn "Love Came Down at Christmas" (*The United Methodist Hymnal*, 242) What connections do you make between this Scripture and the hymn?

4. In what way do you think love is more powerful than fame, force, or money?

5. How have you experienced the power of love at work in your life or in the life of someone you know?

Prayer

O God, help me to see and to believe that love is the most powerful force in all of your creation. Help me to find ways, day by day, to love others as you love us. In Christ, I pray. Amen.

Focus for the Week

We find Bethlehem when we discover the strength and power of love given to us through Jesus Christ. This week, look for ways the power of love is at work in your life. Consider how you might demonstrate love in your words and actions to others.

Daily Devotions

Read the Scriptures for the daily devotions and reflect on what they say to you about the power of love. Record your insights in the space provided.

Day One
Exodus 34:1-9

The Character of God

What can we learn about God's character in Exodus 34:1-9? This Scripture passage is the fourth and final theophany, or appearance of God, in the stories of Exodus. The others occur in Exodus 3:1—4:23; 19:16-19; and 24:15-18. In Chapters 3 and 34, God appears to Moses alone; and in these appearances, Moses learns God's name and God's character. In Exodus 34:1-9, after God has freed the people from slavery in Egypt and provided for them in the wilderness, we learn that God—whose name means "I am who I am" and "I will be who I will be" (3:13-15; 34:5-6)—is One who shows mercy and grace, who is slow to anger, who is filled with love and faithfulness, and who forgives (verses 5-7). While the people will suffer consequences from sin, God's unending and ever-present love make it possible to renew their relationship with God. God's love and faithfulness never ends. These character traits give substance and content to the divine name revealed by God.

What does Exodus 34:1-9 say to you about the love of God? How does it inspire you? How does it challenge you?

Where do you need to practice a deeper level of mercy, love, and forgiveness toward family members, friends, or acquaintances during the week ahead?

Day Two
Psalm 33

Sing About God's Steadfast Love

Psalm 33 is a communal celebration of the character of God as revealed in Creation, in history, and in God's relationship with humanity. God's Word is upright. God does everything with faithfulness. God loves righteousness and justice. The entire earth reveals God's love.

These realities about God's character inspire song and celebration. But the psalm calls for more. Singing and celebration move into awe of God. We are called to trust and hope in God. When we go through hard times or when we have questions about God's presence, the psalm helps us to remember that the God who created everything and who has been with us throughout history is with us now. God will not abandon us because God loves us. Surely this is something to sing about.

How do you see God's love and faithfulness in your
day-to-day life? How was God with you during a hard
time in your life?

What experiences of God's presence challenge or inspire you to celebrate or sing about God's steadfast love?

Day Three
John 1:1, 14-18

The Incarnation

When we say that love came down at Bethlehem, we are close to understanding the Incarnation. In John 1:1, 14-18, we learn that God's eternal word became flesh in Jesus Christ. The Greek for *word* is *logos*, and it carries other meanings in addition to the spoken word. It also means the creative and ordering mind of God. In John's Gospel, this Word is Jesus Christ, who is the power and wisdom of God among us. Jesus reveals and embodies God's love in grace and truth: "No one has ever seen God. It is God the only Son, who is close to the Father's heart, who has made him known" (verse 18). The purpose of Jesus' ministry is to make God known. If we want to know God, we look at Jesus. What we see is love.

What challenges or inspires you about John's understanding of the Incarnation? How do you see the power and wisdom of God in Jesus?

What do you learn about God by looking at Jesus? How do you see the gift of love in Jesus Christ?

Day Four
John 3:16-17

For God So Loved . . .

John's Gospel describes the profound love of God for the entire world in what may be the most familiar verse in the New Testament: "For God so loved the world that he gave his only Son, so that everyone who believes in him may not perish but may have eternal life" (verse 16). Eternal life means so much more than being immortal or having a future life in heaven. It is not something for which we must wait. It also means living now, day by day, in the never-ending presence of God. It carries the possibility for abundance and fullness of life as we move through all its ups and downs. God's purpose for the world is not to condemn the world but to offer life. We discover that life by believing in Jesus Christ, and believing means more than saying something is true. To believe means to trust, to commit, and to give ourselves fully in faith and love to Jesus Christ.

Write John 3:16 below, but write your name in place of the word *world*. Read it aloud. What feelings or thoughts does this evoke for you?

_____

_____

_____

_____

_____

_____

_____

_____

_____

_____

_____

_____

_____

_____

_____

_____

_____

_____

_____

_____

_____

_____

_____

_____

_____

How do you understand the concept of eternal life? What does it mean to you that you can live now in the never-ending presence of God? How does this possibility demonstrate God's love?

Day Five
1 John 4:7-12

God Is Love

Love one another. Live in love. Love is from God.
God is love. This is heady stuff! Our capacity to love
comes from God. When we live in love, we reveal God's
nature. This Scripture goes even further. It boldly asserts
that God is love! The beauty of this Scripture is that
making this assertion calls for response from human
beings. We are called to love one another because when
we do, we reveal God to one another. And there is more.
God is with us. God lives in us and among as, and God's
love is at work through us. "No one has ever seen God;
if we love one another, God lives in us, and his love is
perfected in us" (verse 12). How do we know this reality
about who God is and how God works? We know through
his Son, Jesus Christ.

What do you feel or think about the assertion that God is love? In what ways does this assertion challenge or inspire you to love others?

In the week ahead, how can you put love into practice in a way that others will know God's presence and activity?

Day Six
Romans 8:31-39

God Is for Us

The core truth of the gospel is found in Romans 8:31: "God is for us." Paul builds upon this core truth to help us understand what it means. As it was for Paul and for the early followers of Jesus Christ, our life is full of hardships. God, who loves us, will never abandon us. Jesus Christ proves this love through his ministry, death, and resurrection. He does not condemn us. He loves us and intercedes for us (verse 34). If we don't already understand it, we hear it almost in shouts in the closing verses of this passage. Whatever happens, we are "more than conquerors through him who loved us" (verse 37). No hardship on earth can do away with God's love for us in Jesus Christ. Paul says, "For I am convinced that neither death, nor life, nor angels, nor rulers, nor things present, nor things to come, nor powers, nor height, nor depth, nor anything else in all creation, will be able to separate us from the love of God in Christ Jesus our Lord" (verses 38-39).

What does it mean to you that God is for you? What difference does that truth make in your daily life?

How have you seen God's love at work for you during times of hardship or pain?

4

The Precious Memories
of Christmas

Scripture: Luke 2

If I were to ask you to name your favorite Christmas memory, what would it be? What would you say? Would it be the memory of your mother baking Christmas cookies in the kitchen; or of your dad making a stand for the Christmas tree? Would it be the beautiful sound of a favorite Christmas carol, or the distinctive fragrance of Christmas evergreens in your home? Would it be the memory of a live manger scene, or your first kiss under the mistletoe? Would it be a special present you received, or one you gave? Would it be the memory of celebrating Christmas Eve Communion at church, or hearing your grandfather read Luke's Christmas story to all the family gathered in front of the fireplace? Would it be the time you went to Colorado for a white Christmas and then wrote the words *Santa, we're here* in the snow to help the children rest easy and be confident that Santa could indeed find them even though they were away from home? Would it be the remembrance of Christmas in a foreign land during a year when you could not make it home for the holidays? Or would it be the memory of a great choir singing "The Hallelujah Chorus" in a majestic Christmas concert in a beautiful sanctuary; or of young carolers singing "Silent Night" off-key at your front door?

One Christmas when I was young, my brother, sister, and I announced that we would make all the ornaments for our tree and would decorate the tree from top to bottom with only our homemade ornaments. We made the decorations using paper, pictures, candy, popcorn, and cranberries. An outsider would have been underwhelmed by the sight of that tree. But, without question, our parents thought it was the most beautiful Christmas tree they had ever seen!

Christmas memories. No other season, no other time of the year touches our hearts quite like Christmas. In 1975, Natalie Sleeth wrote a beautiful song entitled "Christmas Is a Feeling" that expresses how Christmas affects people. The song says, "Christmas is a feeling filling the air, / it's love and joy and laughter of people ev'rywhere."

Christmas memories. Oh, how they stir our souls! When you stop to think about it, memory is a wonderful gift God has given us. It's the way we learn and the way we celebrate, and—as amnesia dramatically demonstrates—it is absolutely crucial for our sense of personal identity. Our ancestors in the faith (both the ancient Hebrews and the early Christians) were aware of the importance of memory, which is why we have seasons and traditions, festivals, symbols, colors, and special days. All of these traditions remind us of who we are and whose we are.

Christmas evokes powerful memories and with good reason. That's precisely what it's supposed to do! That's what it's designed to do. That's why we have it. Christmas reminds us that God cares for and watches over us. It reminds us about the real priorities of life, priorities such as love, joy, peace, justice, goodness, kindness, goodwill, grace, forgiveness, and the importance of family, friends, and church. And above all, it reminds us of what God is like and what God wants *us* to be like. Once each year, Christmas comes around to remind us of the things that truly matter.

A quote broadly attributed to the writer Samuel Johnson says, "It is insufficiently considered that men more often require to be reminded than informed." Well, how is your memory? Do you have a good memory? Most of us confess that we don't. Several years ago, I took a memory course. After the final session, they gave us a booklet that was designed to help us reinforce, internalize, and implement all the good things we learned in that course to improve our memories. I'm sure that booklet on memory would be a great help to me, but I can't for the life of me remember where I put it!

Most of us have trouble remembering things from time to time. That's why we need a little Christmas every now and then—to wake us up, to bring us back, to jog our memories, to remind us again of what this life is all about.

Now, with that in mind, let me underscore three things that Christmas helps us to remember: We need a Savior. We have a Savior. We can share the Savior. Let's take a look at these together.

Christmas Reminds Us That We Need a Savior

Oh, how we need a Savior! The name *Jesus* literally means "The Lord is Salvation," "Yahweh Saves," or "Savior." Jesus came at Christmas to do for us what we cannot do for ourselves. He came to save us from our sins.

Outside of the Bible, the most famous Christmas story is *A Christmas Carol* by Charles Dickens. Most everyone knows that Charles Dickens' story is about a gruff, miserly character named Ebenezer Scrooge. We also recall that, in the story, there is a little boy with a disability named Tiny Tim Cratchit who is always saying, "God bless us, every one!" Actually, it's a story about conversion, and did Scrooge ever need converting! He was a despicable character—a selfish, arrogant, hard-hearted, mean-spirited, uncaring, unsympathetic, unchristian tightwad. "Bah! Humbug!" his now-famous response to Christmas, has become the sad theme of his sick spirit.

As the story unfolds, Ebenezer Scrooge is visited one night by some ghosts who subject him to a haunting that few characters in fiction have experienced. Scared by the ghosts, Scrooge is forced to see himself as he really is. The visits of the ghosts and the Christlike unconditional love of the Cratchit family (who keep loving him, even though he has treated them horribly) combine to convert Ebenezer Scrooge.

After he is given a second chance, he changes completely! A skinflint no more, he becomes a loving, generous person. He loves Christmas now. He gets into the spirit of the season by sending presents to the Cratchits and a large amount of money to charity. He dresses up and goes to his nephew's house for Christmas dinner and announces that he is giving his clerk, Bob Cratchit, a nice raise. Talk about a conversion! Talk about a life redeemed and saved!

Why are we so fascinated with this story? It's not just that it's a well-written, classic piece of literature. It's something more: This is our story. Deep down inside, deeper than some of us even realize, we all relate to Ebenezer Scrooge. We all need help. We all have our clay feet. We all need to be converted from selfishness to love. To put it more dramatically, we all need a Savior.

Two thousand years ago, God looked down and saw the sick, Scrooge-like spirit of the world and knew that it needed to change. God sent the Son to save us, change us, and show us a better way. Once a year, Christmas comes around again to jog our memories and to remind us how much we need a Savior.

Christmas Reminds Us That We Have a Savior

I have a friend who was a prisoner of war in Vietnam for over two years. It was an indescribably horrendous, dehumanizing experience that only his solid and deep faith enabled him to survive. He told me that throughout that long, awful, horrible period as a prisoner of war, the one thing that saved his health and sanity was the strong sense of Christ's presence with him. The enemy could take away his freedom. They could take away his fellow Americans. They could take away his food and his dignity. But, the one thing they couldn't take away from him was his Savior and the strong sense of Christ's presence. He said, "Death called to me from every direction. It was in the air I breathed, but somehow I was serene and confident because I knew Christ was with me. Even if death came, Christ would be there with me too! I kept remembering how Paul put it: Nothing, not even death, can separate us from the love of God in Christ Jesus" (see Romans 8:38-39).

That is the good news of our faith, isn't it? That is indeed the good news of Christmas. The angel told the shepherds, "Do not be afraid; for see—I am bringing you good news of great joy for all the people: to you is born this day in the city of David a Savior, who is the Messiah, the Lord" (Luke 2:10-11).

No matter what circumstances we find ourselves in, we can count on this good news. We don't need to be afraid. We have a Savior. Christmas reminds us that we need a Savior and that we have one!

Christmas Reminds Us That We Can Share the Savior

The Christ Child comes at Christmas to show us what God is like and what God wants *us* to be like. The word to describe this image is *love*. Love came down at Christmas. Every time we show love for another person, we are living in the spirit of Christ, we are sharing the Savior, and we are keeping alive the power of Christmas.

As mentioned earlier I'm a fan of the *Peanuts* comic strip. One of my favorites is the one where Lucy decides that Linus (her younger brother) has to grow up and learn to live without his security blanket. So, when Linus falls asleep, she slips the blanket out of his hands, takes it outside, and buries it in the ground. When Linus wakes up and discovers that his blanket is missing, he panics and falls to the floor. He can't get his breath. He gasps and then screams, "Tell me where you buried it! Tell me! . . . I'll die without that blanket!"

Then Snoopy, the dog, sees Linus' dilemma and rises to the occasion. He goes outside and with his trusty nose sniffs out the blanket, digs it up, and brings it back to Linus. Linus is relieved and grateful. With one arm he grabs the blanket and with the other he hugs Snoopy saying, "You found it! You found it!" The last picture shows Snoopy lying on his back on his doghouse with a contented look and thinking, "Every now and then I feel that my existence is justified!"

Love is indeed the justification of our existence. Every time we reach out to help others in the spirit of Christ;

every time we show kindness in the spirit of Christ; every time we express love, we are sharing the Savior. We are living in the spirit of Christmas.

Christmas memories. So many of them touch our hearts and warm our souls. I hope and pray this year that above all else we will remember these three truths: We need a Savior! We have a Savior! And, we can share the Savior!

Questions for Reflection and Discussion

1. What are your favorite memories of Christmas? Why are they special to you? What symbols and traditions are included in your Christmas memories?

2. Do you ever have trouble remembering things? What do you do to help you remember?

3. How does the story of Ebenezer Scrooge in *A Christmas Carol* speak to you about the need for a savior?

4. When has your own awareness of having a Savior helped you through a difficult time in your life?

5. How do you respond to the idea that love is the justification of our existence? What feelings or thoughts do you have about this idea? How do you think love reveals and shares the Savior?

Prayer

Loving and saving God, help us to remember the reason for Christmas. Help us to remember that we need a savior and that we have a Savior. Help us love so that others will know the Savior. In Christ we pray. Amen.

Focus for the Week

We find Bethlehem when we remember that Jesus Christ was born to save us and that he reveals who God is and who we can be. During the week ahead, identify ways to help you remember what God says to you through the birth of Jesus. Take time to listen to music, create art, read the Bible or other devotional material, or simply be quiet so that you can remember who God is and how God reveals God's love and salvation through Jesus Christ.

Daily Devotions

Read the Scriptures for the daily devotions and reflect on what they say to you about remembering God's love and salvation during this Christmas season. Record your insights in the space provided.

Day One
Exodus 13:3-10

Remember This Day

Chapter 13 opens with the details of the Festival of the Unleavened Bread. This festival celebrates the Exodus from Egypt and was intended to be a reminder for the people that God had set them free from slavery. Moses tells the people, "Remember this day on which you came out of Egypt, out of the house of slavery, because the LORD brought you out from there by strength of hand; no leavened bread shall be eaten" (verse 3). He then gives specific instructions for how and when to celebrate the festival. After the instructions, he tells them that the festival is not only for them. "You shall tell your child on that day, 'It is because of what the LORD did for me when I came out of Egypt'" (verse 8). From generation to generation, the festival is intended to remind them that God is present with them and that God saves them.

Why do you think the people of Israel needed a festival to help them remember that God saved them from slavery in Egypt? What connections do you see between this story and the traditions of Christmas?

Do you have family stories that you remember from generation to generation? If so, why are they important to you? What do you want the next generation in your family to remember?

Day Two
Deuteronomy 4:29-31

God Will Not Forget You

As the people stand on the edge of the Promised Land, Moses speaks about their rebellion and commands them to obey God's covenant with them. In Deuteronomy 4, he reminds them that in spite of their disobedience, they will find God if they seek God. "Because the LORD your God is a merciful God, he will neither abandon you nor destroy you; he will not forget the covenant with your ancestors that he swore to them" (verse 31). While they might forget God, God will not forget them or the promises made to their ancestors. The words resonate through the centuries to our ears. We might forget God; but God, who is merciful, will never forget us. God remembers us.

Have you ever felt abandoned or forgotten by God? What was it like?

When have you experienced God's mercy and
faithfulness? What does it mean to you to hear that God
remembers you?

Day Three
Psalm 77

A Help in Troubled Times

Psalms 77 poignantly describes the psalmist's spiritual distress. Despite incessant prayer and meditation, he feels no relief. Instead, he loses sleep and struggles with terrifying questions. Has God abandoned him? Is God angry? Has God stopped loving him? Will God forget God's promises?

Then the psalmist's mood changes as he remembers the stories of the past. It is almost as though the questions themselves evoke the memories of who God is and what God has done in the past. "I will call to mind the deeds of the LORD; I will remember your wonders of old" (verse 11). As the psalmist remembers, a sense of peace returns.

When have you had questions about God? What were your questions? What was it like to ask such questions?

What do you remember about God's presence during troubling times? How do such memories help you?

Day Four
Psalm 103

Do Not Forget

"Bless the LORD, O my soul, and do not forget all his benefits" (verse 2). The psalmist's advice in this verse points toward the value and benefit of remembering God's extravagant mercy and love. As we read the psalm, we may feel that we have encountered an ancient therapy for healing the emotions, not unlike contemporary therapies that involve changing how we think. The psalm calls us to bless God, beginning with ourselves and extending to all creation like ripples in water. God forgives, heals, and redeems. God offers vindication and justice. God's love and compassion endure forever. Remembering and blessing God for these essential traits of God's character offer us the opportunity to experience hope and wonder. Remembering who God is and what God does enriches and nurtures our growth in faith.

What attribute of God's nature means the most to you?
What does it mean to you to remember that God is
merciful and loving?

What events in your life have caused you to glimpse God's love and mercy? What can you do in the week ahead to intentionally remember God's love and mercy? What difference might it make in your life?

Day Five
Luke 22:14-20

In Remembrance of Me

Jesus and the disciples gather in Jerusalem to celebrate the Passover meal. The traditional meal helps them remember that God saved them from oppression in Egypt (see Exodus 12). On this occasion, Jesus gives additional meaning to the bread and the cup. "Then he took a loaf of bread, and when he had given thanks, he broke it and gave it to them, saying, 'This is my body, which is given for you. Do this in remembrance of me.' And he did the same with the cup after supper, saying, 'This cup that is poured out for you is the new covenant in my blood'" (verses 19-20).

God saved the people and gave them freedom through the Exodus experience. In this context of salvation and freedom, Jesus finds a way to help them remember that God's saving activity continues through Jesus' own suffering and sacrifice. The new covenant confirms God's continuing covenant with all of creation. The family of followers will learn that life lived according to God's rule calls for servanthood and love.

Read Exodus 12—13, and then read Luke 22:14-20. What
connections do you see? What do they say to you about
God? about God's expectations for us?

_____

_____

_____

_____

_____

_____

_____

_____

_____

_____

_____

_____

_____

_____

_____

_____

_____

_____

_____

_____

_____

_____

_____

_____

What thoughts or insights come to you about the celebration of the Lord's Supper? How does the meal inspire or challenge you?

Day Six
2 Timothy 1:3-10

God's Grace in Our Savior

Second Timothy 1:3-10 offers inspiring words of gratitude and encouragement to Timothy. Paul remembers Timothy's faith, which was nurtured by his grandmother Lois and his mother Eunice. Faith does not come to us in a vacuum. We grow in it. We are nurtured in it by those around us who teach us and reveal it to us with their lives. Paul moves from remembering to reminders. "Rekindle the gift of God that is within you," he writes (verse 6). What is this gift? It is a spirit of power, love, and self-discipline. He reminds Timothy to rely on God's power. God saves us and calls us to live in God's mercy and love. This salvation and calling is not our doing but comes through God's grace.

Then Paul writes what may be an excerpt from a hymn or a creed among early believers. "This grace was given to us in Christ Jesus before the ages began, but it has now been revealed through the appearing of our Savior Christ Jesus, who abolished death and brought life and immortality to light through the gospel" (verses 9-10). What we discover when we find Bethlehem is a Savior who gives us life!

Who has nurtured your faith in the way Timothy's grandmother and mother nurtured his faith? In what ways?

How do you experience the gift of God's power, love, and self-discipline in your life? In what ways do you think you can rekindle this gift within you?

5

Mind the Light

Scripture: John 1:1-5

When the writers of the Bible tried to express the inexpressible, they used analogies, stories, or comparisons to make their points. When the truth that they wanted to express was too big for words, they searched for dramatic illustrations that could somehow convey the heart of their message. That's what we find in our Scripture lesson for this chapter. How do you express the birth of Jesus Christ to our world? How do you do justice to his birth? How do you capture its impact? How do you communicate what it means? Words were inadequate, so they tried to express it through dramatic poetic analogy. They compared it to light coming into the world of darkness! Now, that's a dramatic way to put it, isn't it? It was dark, and then light came. It was dark, and the light turned on. God's light came into our dark world.

The Gospel of John expresses it well: "The light shines in the darkness, and the darkness did not overcome it" (verse 5). That's what Christmas is about; and that's why it is the season of lights. Everywhere you look—in our cities, our nations, and across the globe—Christmas lights are coming on—lights on Christmas trees and manger scenes, lights on houses and buildings, lights on bushes and hedges, lights on doorways and in windows, candlelights, spotlights, and neon lights. All these lights symbolize the same thing, the light of God coming to a dark world, the light of God coming in the birth of a baby to bring truth, hope, love, and peace to a needy, dusky world.

As I considered this powerful illustration, of God's light coming into the world and of how much we love the lights of Christmas, my mind darted back to a story I had read a few years ago, a true story about a woman named Kate Walker.

Kate was living in Sandy Hook, New Jersey, when she first met Jacob Walker. He was the keeper of the Sandy Hook Lighthouse. They fell in love, and he took her there as his bride. She was so happy there at Sandy Hook because she and Jacob were in love and the lighthouse was on land. In addition to helping him with the lighthouse, she also kept a garden and raised vegetables and flowers. It was a wonderful life.

But then, her husband was transferred to Robbins Reef, a lighthouse in the ocean and surrounded by water. At first, she refused to unpack her trunks and boxes because she was upset about the isolation. But over time, little by little she unpacked, arranged, decorated, and settled in. She loved Jacob dearly, and each day she helped him with the lighthouse duties to the point that she became as proficient at the job as he was. They both knew full well how the ships at sea depended on them. In their work, they were saving lives daily by warning the ships of danger and guiding them to a safe harbor.

One day, Jacob caught a cold while tending the light. His cold turned into pneumonia. Eventually, he became so ill that it was necessary to take him to the hospital where he could receive better care. There was no one else to tend the light. He urged Kate to stay there at the lighthouse and continue his work. She wanted to go with him to the hospital, but he insisted that she stay behind to mind the light. Reluctantly, she agreed. His last words to her were, "Mind the light, Kate."

A few nights later, while Kate tended the light, she saw a boat coming. Something told her what news it was bringing. Somehow she knew something was wrong. She could feel it in the air, and she braced herself for the news that reached her from the darkness: Her husband was dead. After the funeral, Kate stayed on at the lighthouse.

I remember reading Kate's poignant words: "Every morning when the sun comes up, I stand at the porthole and look towards his grave. Sometimes the hills are brown, sometimes they are green, sometimes they are white with snow. But always they bring a message from him, something I heard him say more often than anything else. Just three words: 'Mind the light!'"[1]

That story is something of a Christmas parable for us, isn't it? A strong message always seems to come to us when we look toward the manger in Bethlehem. From the manger of Bethlehem and from the empty tomb of Jerusalem come those three powerful words: "Mind the light!" That is, keep the light of Christ aglow in this world. Keep bright and clear and visible what Jesus stood for and lived for. Keep bright and clear and visible what he believed in and died for. Mind the light! Keep the light of Christmas burning.

When we find Bethlehem in the midst of the bedlam in our world, we find God's light in Jesus Christ. Our job as Christians is to be reflectors of the light of Christ and to bring some measure of his light and life to dark corners of the world. As we celebrate Christmas this year, it is my prayer that each one of us who finds Bethlehem will "mind the light": the Light of Peace, the Light of Hope, the Light of Love.

Mind the Light of Peace

At the first Christmas, Christ came into the world as the Prince of Peace, calling for peace on earth and goodwill toward all people. In our rapidly shrinking world, it is becoming more and more evident with every passing day what Christmas tried to teach us long ago through a newborn baby in a manger in Bethlehem. We are a family. We are brothers and sisters with all the people of the world. As the apostle Paul put it in his famous sermon in front of the Areopagus in Athens: "From one ancestor [God] made all nations to inhabit the whole earth" (Acts 17:26). This is the strong message of Christmas that we must not miss, the good news given by the angel who appeared to the shepherds: "'Do not be afraid; for see—I am bringing you good news of great joy for all the people: to you is born this day in the city of David a Savior, who is the Messiah, the Lord. This will be a sign for you: you will find a child wrapped in bands of cloth and lying in a manger.' And suddenly there was with the angel a multitude of the heavenly host, praising God and saying, 'Glory to God in the highest heaven, and on earth peace among those whom he favors!'" (Luke 2:10-14).

Whenever and wherever people are working for peace, there is the spirit of Christmas. I think God has a special love for peacemakers. Jesus put it like this: "Blessed are the peacemakers, for they will be called children of God" (Matthew 5:9). In their song the hymn writers Sy Miller and Jill Jackson expressed it like this: "Let there be peace on earth, and let it begin with me."

The point is clear. Whether it's the world scene, the national level, a schoolyard, an office discussion, a neighborhood disagreement, or a family confrontation, God has a special love for the peacemaker. Every year, Christmas comes around to remind us of that. If you want to please God, if you want to find Bethlehem and live in the light of Christmas, then be a peacemaker wherever you are. Mind the light of peace.

Mind the Light of Hope

In his book *The Miracle of Hope*, Dr. Charles L. Allen writes about a US submarine that sank off the coast of

Massachusetts, thus becoming a prison for its crew. Divers went down to help. They heard a sound from inside the sunken sub. The trapped sailors, short on oxygen, were tapping Morse code on the side of the submarine. It was a question: "Is . . . there . . . any . . . hope?"[2] Is there any hope? Christmas answers that question with a resounding "Yes!" Christ comes into the world as the Prince of Peace and as the Savior, the Hope of the world.

I once heard a story about a group of ministers who were meeting in a hotel in Chicago when a fire broke out. The ministers were close to panic as flames and smoke blocked the normal escape routes through the corridor to the stairway. They rushed out onto a balcony to escape the smoke, but they were ten stories up. There was no escape that way. Then one of the ministers braved the smoke and went back through the room where they had been meeting until he found an exit to a fire escape. He then returned for the others and led them to safety. Later, one of the other ministers said, "You cannot imagine the feeling of relief in hearing and seeing that man come back to us and say, 'This way out,' and to see him point the way to safety." The good news of Christmas is that God cares for us so much that God comes to save us.

Every year, Christmas comes around to remind us of that. We find Bethlehem when we claim the hope offered by the God who saves us through Jesus Christ. If you want to please God, if you want to live in the light of Christmas, accept Christ as your Savior and as the hope of your world and share that hope with others. Mind the light of peace and the light of hope.

Mind the Light of Love

In the fifth century, a monk named Telemachus had spent most of his days in prayer, fasting, and meditation while in retreat from the world. But one day, he sensed that God wanted him to go to Rome. When he arrived in Rome, he saw a large crowd of people filing into an amphitheater. Telemachus also went in to see what was happening. Thousands of people were jammed into the amphitheater to watch the gladiator contests. Telemachus had no idea what was about to happen. He had never seen anything like that.

Suddenly, the gladiators entered the arena to the roar of the crowd. Telemachus shuddered. He had never heard of gladiator games before, but he had a premonition of horrible violence. When the games began, Telemachus was horrified. For the amusement of the crowd, men were brutally killing one another. Telemachus couldn't stand it. He jumped on the perimeter wall and shouted, "In the name of Christ, stop!" No one paid him any attention. Suddenly, Telemachus jumped into the arena, ran over, stood between the gladiators, and said, "In the name of Christ, stop!" They pushed him aside as the crowd laughed. But Telemachus was persistent. They would push him away, but he would scramble back and stand in between the gladiators, begging them to stop. Traditional retellings of the story report that someone killed the monk with a sword; and one by one, the people in the crowd left the coliseum. Theodoret of Cyrus reported that the infuriated crowd stoned Telemachus to death. According to legend, this event prompted the emperor Honorius to end the vicious games. Telemachus stood tall for love! It cost him his life, but he stood tall for love.

That's what Christ did. He came into a brutal world with a message of love. He came into a hostile arena and stood tall for love. And now that is our calling. Every year, Christmas comes around to remind us of that. When we stand tall for love, we find Bethlehem. If you want to please God, if you want to live in the spirit of Christmas, then stand tall for love. Mind the light of peace, the light of hope, and the light of love.

[1] From "Lighthouse Kate," Staten Island History website, http:www. statenislandhistory.com/si-lighthouse.html (accessed Jun 06, 2013).

[2] From *The Miracle of Hope*, by Charles Livingston Allen (Fleming H. Revell Company, 1973); page 11.

Questions for Reflection and Discussion

1. Read John 1:1-5. What thoughts, feelings, or insights do you have about this Scripture? How does the image of light speak to you about God's presence with us in Jesus Christ?

2. How does Kate Walker's story speak to you about "minding the light" of Christ in our world?

3. What opportunities do you see for minding the light of peace personally, nationally, and globally? What inspires you or discourages you about possibilities for peace? How does the birth of Jesus Christ offer the gift of peace?

4. Where do you see hope in our world? How do you think the saving love of God in Jesus Christ offers hope? In what ways do you think you can mind the light of hope?

5. In what ways can you mind the light of love in your family? among your friends? in your community? in our world?

Prayer

God of all people and all creation, help us find Bethlehem in the bedlam of our lives. Open our eyes and our hearts to the light of Jesus Christ in our midst. Guide us as we mind the light of your peace, hope, and love. Amen.

Closing Reflection

In this study, we have explored several important aspects of how we can find Bethlehem in the midst of the bedlam in our lives. We all know that bedlam in all its shapes and forms is unavoidable, whether it is the bedlam of daily busyness or the bedlam of traumatic events. In all these circumstances, finding Bethlehem means finding the presence of God in Jesus Christ. We find Bethlehem in the midst of bedlam when we discover the freedom, hope, peace, love, life, and salvation given to us through Jesus Christ.

As we celebrate the birth of Jesus in Bethlehem, we remember these gifts. We remember that we are not alone. We remember that God is with us. Finding Bethlehem leads to another important step in our lives of faith; it inspires us to share this good news with others through our words and through our actions. God calls us to "mind the light" of love through Jesus Christ.

Also Part of the FINDING BETHLEHEM IN THE MIDST OF BEDLAM *Study:*

- FINDING BETHLEHEM IN THE MIDST OF BEDLAM: AN ADVENT STUDY FOR YOUTH (9781426768996)
- FINDING BETHLEHEM IN THE MIDST OF BEDLAM: AN ADVENT STUDY FOR CHILDREN (9781426769016)

Other Titles by James W. Moore

Do Your Best and Trust God for the Rest (9781426771866)

Love of a Dad (9781426767456)

Home Is Where Your Mom Is (9781426767982)

Attitude Is Your Paintbrush (9781426753947)

Come on Home (9781426753299)

Daddy Is That Story True, or Were You Just Preaching? (9781426744631)

The Best of James W. Moore (9781426742002)

Yes, Lord, I Have Sinned but I Have Several Excellent Excuses: 20th Anniversay Edition (9781426740978)

I Hear Voices and That's a Good Thing (9781426742163)

Moments That Take Your Breath Away (9780687490691)

Faith Is the Answer, But What Are the Questions? (9780687646739)

Rich in the Things That Count the Most (9780687490103)

There's a Hole in Your Soul That Only God Can Fill (9780687054565)

If You're Going the Wrong Way . . . Turn Around! (9780687006885)

Noah Built His Ark in the Sunshine (9780687075386)

If God Has a Refrigerator, Your Picture Is on It (9780687026814)

At the End of the Day (9780687045136)

God Was Here and I Was Out to Lunch (9780687097227)

Seizing the Moments (9780687015528)

Some Folks Feel the Rain, Others Just Get Wet (9780687077540)